Design: Judith Chant and Alison Lee
Recipe Photography: Peter Barry
Jacket and Illustration Artwork: Jane Winton, courtesy of
Bernard Thornton Artists, London
Editor: Josephine Bacon

CHARTWELL BOOKS
a division of Book Sales, Inc.
POST OFFICE BOX 7100
114 Northfield Avenue
Edison, NJ 08818-7100

CLB 4264

Printed and bound in Singapore
ISBN 0-7858-0292-4

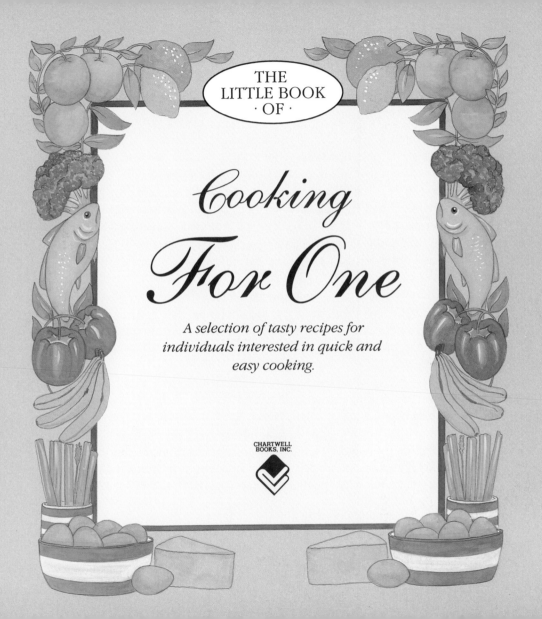

THE LITTLE BOOK · OF ·

Cooking For One

A selection of tasty recipes for individuals interested in quick and easy cooking.

CHARTWELL
BOOKS, INC.

Introduction

Cooking for one sounds easy, but in fact it is often easier to cook a family casserole or pie than it is to make a single portion of a tasty dish. It is just too easy not to bother, and just make do with a sandwich and a piece of cake, or a piece of cheese and an apple, or maybe you get store-bought TV dinners. Sometimes this is all right and is the appropriate thing to do, but on a daily basis it is not good for the morale, and it can lead to a poor and dull diet.

There is a side to cooking that is therapeutic and comforting. There is the planning involved, the shopping, the preparation, and finally the eating and enjoyment of something thoughtfully made. Cooking and eating good food adds an extra dimension to the day whether you are eating alone or with friends.

There are certain aspects of our high-tech modern world that actually make it far easier to shop and cook for one than could be imagined a few years ago. Firstly, there is a greater selection of foods than ever before with a vast array of exotic fruit and vegetables, meat and fish, and spices and grains from all over the world filling our supermarket shelves. Self-service weighing scales are a great boon when buying fruit and vegetables as they enable the shopper to buy the exact amount they require. Also, once home with the shopping the microwave can be of tremendous help for cooking vegetables and reheating previously made dishes. It was always a shame, in the pre-microwave era, when yesterday's succulent fish pie became dry after reheating in the oven. Of course, the freezer has obvious advantages for the single person, too. Delicious bakes, risottos and casseroles can be made, divided into single portions and frozen for later use.

People cooking for themselves generally do not want to spend too long preparing their meals, and if they are going to cook, they want the result to be something special – that is what this book is all about. The recipes are easy to follow, simple to prepare, and each one has a special ingredient or interesting method to make the dish particularly appetizing. For instance, olives are added to scrambled eggs, lemon is added to sautéed pork, green peppers and tomato go into the ham omelet, fish fillet is pan-blackened with cayenne and paprika, and pancakes are filled with apple. Thus, with today's rich and varied food supply plus the recipes in this book to add the necessary stimulus, those who are cooking for one have no excuse not to eat an exciting and nutritious diet.

Scrambled Eggs with Olives

SERVES 1

The addition of black olives to scrambled eggs turns this simple dish into a memorable one.

PREPARATION: 10 mins
COOKING: 15 mins

---

3 eggs
2 tbsps olive oil
¼ small onion, chopped
1 small clove garlic, chopped
1 tomato, seeded and finely chopped
4 black olives, pitted and finely chopped
Butter
Salt and pepper

---

1. Beat the eggs and set them aside.

2. Warm the olive oil in a small skillet, increase the heat to high and cook the onion, garlic, tomato, and olives until all the juices have evaporated.

3. Heat a little butter in a small saucepan, add the eggs and cook over a gentle heat, stirring continuously with a wooden spoon.

4. Once the eggs are cooked, stir in the tomato

Step 3 Cook the eggs over a gentle heat, stirring continuously with a wooden spoon.

Step 4 Once the eggs are cooked, stir in the tomato and olive mixture.

and olive mixture. Heat through and serve immediately.

Omelet Rousillon

MAKES 1 OMELET

Rousillon is a region of France near the Spanish border. The Spanish influence is evident in the use of tomatoes and peppers combined with eggs.

PREPARATION: 15 mins
COOKING: 5 mins

---

3 eggs
Salt and pepper
1 tbsp butter or margarine
¼ green bell pepper, cut into small dice
½ cup diced ham
2 tomatoes, peeled, seeded, and coarsely
   chopped

---

1. Break the eggs into a bowl, season with salt and pepper, and beat to mix thoroughly. Heat an omelet pan or small skillet and add the

Step 2 Push eggs with fork to let the uncooked portion run to the bottom of the pan.

Step 3 Fold a third of the omelet to the middle.

butter, swirling it so that it coats the bottom and sides. When the butter stops foaming, add the pepper and ham. Cook 1-2 minutes to soften slightly, and add the tomatoes.

2. Pour in the eggs and as they begin to cook, push back the cooked portion with the flat of the fork to allow the uncooked portion to run underneath. Continue to lift the eggs and shake the pan to prevent them from sticking.

3. When the egg on top is still slightly creamy, fold a third of the omelet to the center and tip it out of the pan onto a warm serving dish, folded side down. Serve immediately.

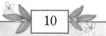

Lamb Korma

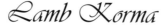

SERVES 1

One of the best known Indian curries, a korma is rich, spicy and a traditional favorite.

PREPARATION: 15 mins
COOKING: 50 mins

½ small onion, sliced
2 tsps vegetable oil
Piece of cinnamon stick
2 cloves
1 cardamom pod
½ bayleaf
¼ tsp black cumin seeds
½ tsp ginger paste, or grated fresh ginger
¼ tsp garlic paste, or 1 small clove garlic,
   crushed
1 cup cubed lean shoulder of lamb
¼ tsp chili powder
¼ tsp ground coriander
½ tsp ground cumin
Pinch of ground turmeric
2 tbsps plain yogurt
⅓ cup water
Salt to taste
1 tsp ground almonds
½ green chili, seeded
Fresh coriander (cilantro) leaves, chopped

1. Fry the onion in the oil until golden-brown. Add the cinnamon, cloves, cardamom, bayleaf, and the cumin seeds. Fry 1 minute.

2. Add the ginger and garlic, and the cubed lamb. Sprinkle with the chili powder, ground coriander (cilantro), cumin, and turmeric and mix together well.

3. Stir in the yogurt, cover the pan, and cook over a moderate heat for 10-15 minutes, stirring occasionally.

4. Add the water and salt to taste, re-cover and simmer gently for 30-40 minutes, or until the meat is tender.

5. Just before serving, add the almonds, chili and coriander (cilantro) leaves. Stir in a little more water if necessary, to produce a medium-thick gravy.

Pan-Blackened Fish

SERVES 1

This Cajun recipe uses a very strong spice mixture, so adapt it to your own taste.

PREPARATION: 15 mins
COOKING: 5 mins

---

4 tbsps unsalted butter, melted
1 fish steak about 8 ounces in weight
¾ tsp paprika
¼ tsp garlic granules
¼ tsp cayennne pepper
½ tsp salt and some ground pepper
¼ tsp dried thyme

---

1. Pour about half the melted butter into a small bowl and set aside.

2. Brush the fish steak liberally on both sides with the remaining butter.

3. Mix together the spices, seasonings, and thyme, and sprinkle generously on each side of the steak patting it on by hand.

4. Heat a skillet and add about ½oz butter.

Step 5 Cook the first side until it is very brown then turn over to cook the second side.

When the butter is hot, add the fish.

5. Turn the fish over when the underside is very brown, this should take at least 2 minutes. Repeat with the second side. Add more butter if necessary.

6. Cook until the top side of the fish is very dark brown. Serve the fish immediately with the dish of butter for dipping.

Liver with Onions

SERVES 1

This dish is simple to prepare, yet absolutely delicious and highly nutritious.

PREPARATION: 15 mins
COOKING: 10 mins

1 small onion
5 ounces lambs' liver, thinly sliced
Salt and freshly ground black pepper
3 tbsps all-purpose flour
1½ tbsps vegetable oil
1 tbsp butter
2 tsps fresh minced parsley

1. Peel the onion and slice thinly, keeping each slice whole if possible.

2. Trim away any tubes and connective tissue

Step 1 Peel the onion and slice thinly keeping each slice whole if possible.

Step 3 Coat the liver slices with seasoned flour.

from the liver, using a pair of small scissors or a sharp knife.

3. Mix the seasonings and the flour together on a plate. Lay the slices of liver in the flour, turning them and pressing them gently to coat all over evenly.

4. Put the oil and the butter into a large skillet. Heat gently until foaming.

5. Add the onion rings and fry until just golden.

6. Add the liver slices and fry for 2-3 minutes on each side until just cooked. Cooking time will depend on the thickness of each slice.

7. Stir the parsley into the liver and onions and serve immediately.

Lamb à l'Orange

SERVES 1

The refreshing taste of orange complements lamb beautifully and this recipe is an ideal way of using up leftover lamb.

PREPARATION: 15 mins
COOKING: 18 mins

---

1 tsp oil
1 shallot, finely chopped
1 small orange
1 tsp cranberry jelly
⅓ cup broth
Pinch powder mustard
Pinch of superfine sugar
Pinch of cayenne pepper
1 tsp cornstarch
1 cup cooked lamb

---

1. Heat the oil in a skillet and sauté the shallot gently until soft but not brown.

2. Grate half the orange rind, cut 3 slices from the orange, trim away the white parts and reserve the slices for garnish.

3. Squeeze the juice from the remainder of the orange and add to the shallot, with the orange rind, cranberry jelly, and stock.

Step 2 Cut 3 slices from the orange, trim away the white parts and reserve for garnish.

4. Bring this mixture to the boil, reduce the heat and cook, stirring continuously, 5 minutes.

5. Blend the mustard, sugar, pepper, and cornstarch together with 2 tsps cold water, and stir this into the orange sauce.

6. Slice the lamb, add this to the sauce, and bring to the boil.

7. Reduce the heat and simmer 10-12 minutes. When cooked, transfer the lamb to a serving platter, pour a little of the sauce over it, and garnish with the reserved orange slices.

Chicken and Sausage Risotto

SERVES 1

This is really a one-pot meal and one you won't have to cook in the oven.

PREPARATION: 25 mins
COOKING: 25 mins

---

1 tbsp butter or margarine
½ small onion, coarsely chopped
1 stick celery, roughly chopped
½ small green bell pepper, roughly chopped
1 small clove garlic, crushed
Salt and pepper
2 tbsps uncooked rice
1 small chicken breast, skinned, boned, and cut
    into cubes
⅓ cup canned tomatoes
1 small smoked sausage, cut into
    ½-inch dice
⅔ cup chicken broth
Minced parsley

---

1. Melt the butter or margarine in a large saucepan and add the onion. Cook slowly to brown and then add the celery, green pepper, and garlic and cook briefly.

2. Add the salt and pepper, and the rice, stirring to mix well. Add the chicken, tomatoes, sausage, and broth and mix well.

3. Bring to the boil, then reduce the heat and simmer about 20-25 minutes, stirring occasionally until the chicken is cooked and the rice is tender. The rice should have absorbed most of the liquid by the time it has cooked. Add some minced parsley and serve.

Paprika Schnitzel

SERVES 1

Thin slices of pork fillet are served with a rich-tasting paprika sauce for a delicious low calorie meal.

PREPARATION: 20 mins
COOKING: 15 mins

---

2 thin slices fillet pork, cut along the grain
Salt and freshly ground black pepper
1 small clove garlic, crushed
2 tsps vegetable oil
½ small onion
½ small red bell pepper
½ small green bell pepper
¾ tsp paprika
3 tbsps beef broth
2 tbsps red wine
2 tsps tomato paste
3 tbsps plain yogurt

Step 1 Flatten the pork fillets with a rolling pin or steak hammer until ¼-inch thick.

1. Trim the slices of pork to remove any fat, and flatten them out with a rolling pin until they are ¼-inch thick.

2. Rub both sides of the pork fillets with salt, pepper, and garlic, then refrigerate 30 minutes.

3. Heat the oil in a large skillet and cook the pork fillets until they are well-browned and cooked right through. This will take about 4 minutes for each side.

4. Remove the pork from the pan, set aside, and keep warm.

5. Thinly slice the onion and the peppers. Add to the oil and meat juices in the skillet, and cook quickly for about 3-4 minutes until they are soft but not browned.

6. Add the paprika, stock, wine and tomato paste to the skillet with the vegetables, and bring the mixture to the boil.

7. Reduce the heat and simmer until the liquid has evaporated and the sauce has thickened. Season with salt and pepper to taste.

8. Arrange the pork slices on a serving platter and pour the paprika sauce over them.

9. Beat the yogurt until it is smooth and carefully drizzle over the paprika sauce to make an attractive pattern. Serve hot.

Crunchy Cod

SERVES 1

Cod provides the perfect base for a crunchy, slightly spicy topping.

PREPARATION: 15 mins
COOKING: 12 mins

1 cod fillet
Salt and pepper
2 tbsps melted butter
2 tbsps dry breadcrumbs
¼ tsp powder mustard
¼ tsp crushed garlic
⅛ tsp each of Worcestershire sauce and
    Tabasco
½ tbsp lemon juice
1 tsp minced parsley

Step 1 Season the fish fillet then brush with melted butter.

Step 3 Press the crumbs on gently to pack them in place.

1. Season the fish fillet with salt and pepper and place on a broiler pan. Brush with some of the butter and cook under a medium preheated broiler about 5 minutes.

2. Combine the remaining butter with the breadcrumbs, mustard, garlic, Worcestershire sauce, Tabasco, lemon juice, and parsley.

3. Spoon the mixture carefully on top of the fish fillet, covering it completely. Press down lightly to pack the crumbs into place. Broil for a further 5-7 minutes, or until the top is lightly browned and the fish flakes easily.

Corned Beef Hash

SERVES 1

The addition of cooked beets gives this dish a dash of color.

PREPARATION: 20 mins
COOKING: 30 mins

1 cup canned corned beef
1 medium boiled potato, coarsely chopped
½ small onion, minced
Salt, pepper and nutmeg
1 medium cooked beet, peeled and diced
1 tbsp oil

1. Cut the corned beef into small pieces.

Step 2 Add the meat mixture to the pan and spread it out evenly in the pan.

Step 4 When a crust forms on the bottom, turn the mixture over to brown the other side.

Combine with all the remaining ingredients except the oil.

2. Melt the oil in a skillet and, when hot, add the meat mixture. Spread it out evenly in the pan.

3. Cook over low heat, pressing the mixture down continuously with a wooden spoon or metal spatula. Cook about 15-20 minutes.

4. When a crust forms on the bottom, turn over and brown the other side. Serve on its own or top with a poached egg.

Piquant Pork Chop

SERVES 1

The spicy sauce in this recipe completely transforms the humble pork chop.

PREPARATION: 15 mins
COOKING: 40 mins

---

1 lean pork chop, trimmed of fat and rind
Oil
½ small onion, chopped
1 tsp brown sugar
½-1 tsp mustard powder
½ tsp tomato paste
½ beef stock cube
⅔ cup water
½ tsp Worcestershire sauce
1½ tbsps fresh lemon juice
Sea salt
Freshly-ground black pepper

---

1. Broil the pork chop under a preheated hot broiler for 6-7 minutes on each side.

2. Heat a little oil in a small skillet, and sauté the onion gently until it is lightly browned.

3. Stir the sugar, mustard powder, tomato paste, and beef stock cube into the cooked onion. Mix the ingredients together well, then add the water and bring to the boil, stirring continuously.

4. Stir the Worcestershire sauce and the lemon juice into the onion and spice mixture, then check the seasoning, adding sea salt and black pepper to taste.

5. Put the pork chop into a small ovenproof baking dish and pour the sauce over it.

6. Cook in a preheated oven at 350°F, for about 40-45 minutes, or until the meat is tender.

Ham Steaks with Raisin Sauce

SERVES 1

The sweet-and-sour flavor of this sauce is the perfect choice to complement ham steaks.

PREPARATION: 30 mins
COOKING: 15 mins

2 small ham steaks, cut about ¼-inch thick
Milk
Oil or butter for frying

Sauce
1 tsp cornstarch
6 tbsps cider or apple juice
Large pinch of ground ginger or allspice
1 tsp lemon juice
1 tbsp raisins
Pinch of salt

1. Soak the steaks in enough milk to barely cover them for 30 minutes. Rinse and dry. Trim off any rind and fat and snip the edges of the steaks to prevent curling during cooking.

2. Heat a small amount of oil or butter in a large skillet and brown the steaks for about 2 minutes per side over a medium-high heat.

Step 1 Snip the edges of the ham steaks to prevent the slices from curling.

3. Mix the cornstarch with about 1 tbsp of the cider and deglaze the skillet with the remaining cider. Stir in the ginger or allspice, and the lemon juice.

4. Stirring constantly, add the cornstarch mixture and bring the liquid to the boil. Cook and stir constantly until thickened.

5. Add the raisins and cook for a further 5 minutes. Add salt to taste. Reheat the ham quickly, if necessary, and pour the sauce over the steaks to serve.

Lamb in a Package

SERVES 1

Use this quick and easy recipe to make a whole meal in one convenient package.

PREPARATION: 15 mins
COOKING: 1 hour

---

3 tbsps oil
1 lamb steak or 2 rib chops
1 potato, unpeeled and scrubbed
2 baby carrots, scraped
½ small onion, sliced
½ small green bell pepper, sliced
½ tsp dill seeds
Salt and pepper

---

1. Heat a skillet and add 2 tbsps of oil. Quickly fry the lamb on both sides to sear and brown.

Step 5 Top the lamb with the onion and pepper slices.

Step 6 Sprinkle with dill, salt, and pepper and seal the foil into a parcel.

2. Cut a piece of aluminum foil about 12 × 18 inches and oil lightly.

3. Cut the potato in half and place on the piece of foil, cut side upward.

4. Top with the lamb and place the carrots on either side.

5. Place the onion slices on the lamb and the pepper slices on top of the onions.

6. Sprinkle with the dill, salt, and pepper, and seal the foil into a package.

7. Bake in an oven preheated to 400°F, for about 45 minutes-1 hour, or until the potato is tender and the meat is cooked. Open the package at the table.

Sautéed Lemon Pork

SERVES 1

A perfect way to prepare this tender cut of pork. Butchers will flatten the meat for you, or place it between two sheets of wax paper and beat with a steak hammer.

PREPARATION: 25 mins
COOKING: 25 mins

---

2 lean pork scallops or steaks, beaten until thin
Flour for dredging
Salt and pepper
1 tbsp butter or margarine
½ small green bell pepper, thinly sliced
1 small lemon
1½ tbsps dry white wine or sherry
3 tbsps chicken broth

---

1. Dust the pork with a mixture of flour, salt, and pepper. Shake off the excess.

2. Melt the butter or margarine in a skillet and brown the pork. Remove the meat and keep it warm.

3. Add the pepper to the pan and cook briefly, then set aside with the pork.

4. Cut the lemon in half and squeeze 2 tsps juice from one half. Cut all the peel and white parts from the other half and thinly slice the flesh.

5. Pour the wine or sherry and lemon juice into the pan to deglaze it. Add the broth and bring to the boil. Boil for 2-3 minutes to reduce.

6. Add the pork and peppers and cook 10-15 minutes over gentle heat. Add the lemon slices and heat through before serving.

Beef with Broccoli

SERVES 1

This recipe uses the traditional Chinese method of cutting meat for stir-frying which ensures that the meat will be tender and will cook quickly.

PREPARATION: 25 mins
COOKING: 4 mins

6 ounces rump steak, partially frozen
4 tbsps dark soy sauce
1 tbsp cornstarch
1 tbsp dry sherry
1 tsp sugar
½ cup fresh broccoli
½-inch piece ginger, peeled and shredded
3 tbsps oil
Salt and pepper

1. Trim any fat from the meat and cut into very thin strips across the grain – the strips should be about 3 inches long.

2. Combine the meat with the soy sauce,

Step 1 Slice the meat into thin strips across the grain.

Step 3 Cut the peeled broccoli stalks into thin diagonal slices.

cornstarch, sherry, and sugar. Stir well and leave long enough for the meat to completely defrost.'

3. Break the broccoli into flowerets and cut these into even-sized pieces. Peel the stalks of the broccoli and cut into thin, diagonal slices.

4. Slice the ginger into shreds. Heat a wok and add half of the oil to it. Add the broccoli and sprinkle with salt. Stir-fry, turning constantly, until the broccoli is dark green. Do not cook longer than 2 minutes. Remove from the wok and set aside.

5. Place the remaining oil in the wok and add the ginger and beef. Stir-fry, turning constantly, about 2 minutes. Return the broccoli to the pan and mix well. Heat through for 30 seconds and serve immediately.

Apple-Filled Pancake

SERVES 1

A light, puffy pancake makes a delicious brunch dish as well as a dessert.

PREPARATION: 15 mins
COOKING: 15 mins

Filling
1 tbsp butter or margarine
1 cooking apple, peeled, cored, and cut into
  ¼-inch wedges
1 tsp brown sugar
Pinch of ground allspice

Pancakes
1 egg
½ cup milk
2 tbsp all-purpose flour
¼ tsp sugar
Pinch of salt
1 tbsp butter or margarine
Confectioner's sugar

1. Melt the butter for the filling in a small skillet over moderate heat. When just foaming, add the apple, and sprinkle with the brown sugar and allspice. Cook, stirring occasionally, until the apple is lightly browned and slightly softened. Put the apple aside while preparing the pancake mix.

2. Combine the egg and the milk in a bowl and whisk thoroughly. Sift the flour with the sugar

Step 4 Scatter the apple filling evenly over the pancake.

and salt and add to the egg gradually, whisking constantly. Alternatively, combine all the ingredients in a food processor and work until just smooth.

3. To cook the pancake, melt the butter over moderate heat in a 6-inch skillet. Pour in half the batter and swirl the pan from side to side so that the batter covers the base.

4. Scatter the filling over the pancake and cook about 3 minutes.

5. Pour the rest of the pancake mix over the apples and place under a preheated broiler about 1-2 minutes, or until the top is golden-brown and firm to the touch.

6. Loosen the sides and the base of the pancake and slide it onto a warmed dish. Sprinkle the pancake with a little sifted confectioner's sugar.

Brown Sugar Banana

SERVES 1

Banana cooked in a rich brown sugar sauce makes a delectable dessert.

PREPARATION: 10 mins
COOKING: 8 mins

1 ripe banana, peeled
Lemon juice
2 tbsps butter
1 tbsp soft brown sugar, light or dark
Pinch each of ground cinnamon and nutmeg
2 tbsps orange juice
1 tbsp white or dark rum
Vanilla flavored yogurt and chopped pecans, to
  serve

1. Cut the banana in half lengthwise and sprinkle with lemon juice all over.

2. Melt the butter in a small skillet and add the sugar, cinnamon, nutmeg, and orange juice. Stir over gentle heat until the sugar dissolves into a syrup.

3. Add the banana halves and cook gently about 3 minutes, basting often with the syrup, but not turning them.

4. Once the banana is heated through, warm the rum in a small saucepan, or in a ladle and ignite with a match. Pour the flaming rum over the banana and shake the pan gently until the flames die down naturally. Place on a serving plate and top with some vanilla-flavored yogurt and a sprinkling of pecans.

Brioche French Toast

SERVES 1

This brioche French toast can be served as an unusual dessert, and also as an extra-special breakfast dish, with or without vanilla custard or vanilla yogurt.

PREPARATION: 5 mins
COOKING: 4 mins

---

1 small brioche
1 tbsp heavy cream
1 small egg
1 tsp sugar
¼ tsp orangeflower water
2 tbsps butter
Confectioner's sugar
Vanilla custard sauce or vanilla yogurt, to serve

---

1. Cut the small brioche into three slices.

2. Beat together the cream, egg, sugar, and orangeflower water.

3. Dip each brioche slice into the cream-and-egg mixture, making sure both sides are coated.

4. Heat a little butter and sauté the dipped slices in a skillet about 2 minutes on each side until golden-brown.

Step 3 Dip each brioche slice into the cream and egg mixture, coating both sides.

Step 4 Sauté the dipped slices for about 2 minutes on each side until golden.

5. Serve immediately, sprinkled with a little sifted confectioners sugar and surrounded by the vanilla custard sauce.

Index